Am I Awake, Yet?

Am I Awake, Yet?

Living With a Loved One

That Has Bipolar, And How

To Cope

By: Lisa M. Ashlock

Am I Awake, Yet? **** Living With a Loved One That Has Bipolar, And How to Cope

All material in this book is intended for education only and is not to be used in place of a doctor's care or advice.

Cover design by Alissa Ashlock

Proofreading and Editing by Alissa Ashlock

Published by Main Street Productions

First Printing: May 2017

ISBN 978-1546667391

CONTENTS

INTRODUCTION

~THE FIGHT FROM WITHIN~

I know you feel that I am the helpless one. Believe in me, I say. I am not helpless, I am not dead, I am just hurting inside wanting to say goodbye. I may be alive even though I feel dead inside.

Even though I may be on meds, yes, they do work, however, I still have that feeling that I am dead inside. I feel the pain that you do not. The pain may not be physical, but it's emotional and hurts more sometimes than the physical pain. Physical pain sometimes feels good because it releases the stress from within. I know this is not how I want to live, so I try so hard to be happy, to feel happy, to feel wanted, loved, accomplished, self-confident and worthy.

The darkness seeps inside of me, takes over, and it's a fight to get out of it every day. Every day is a new day for me. I don't know how I am going to feel or what break down I may have. At times, the anxiety gets so high, the depression gets out of control, the torture inside comes over me and I may act out. I try to be perfect, but I am far from it. The feelings within are too deep to explain, the pain, the sadness, the fear, the knowing that I am different and I have to live with this every day of my life. Can I be normal? Will I ever be or feel normal? What is normal?

Life has just begun for me however, it seems as though it's already over.

It's like I have already said my last goodbyes

The pain seems as though it will never go away

The pain will never die

It only hides

Within itself

Alone

I don't seem to hear anyone when they say everything will be ok

I keep waiting for my life to come back the way it once was

I wasn't always this way.

I was normal at one time, happy and outgoing, courageous and confident

Sitting here waiting patiently for the norm to call me

I don't hear your voice at all

The emptiness inside eats me alive

This is what truly lies within a shell

Inside my head everyday

No one to hear me yell

Within this hell

No one hears my cries

No one cares about my demise

Life no longer exist inside this hell

Inside myself

Lord, please help me become myself again

I don't want this hell any longer

I want to be stronger

I want to live longer

    I don't want to stop, but the feelings inside me are telling me to die

Lord, please help me

Lord, I ask you why me

I want to believe

I don't want to leave

I want to be me again

I want to love, feel loved, no more hatred, no more pain

Just to be me again!

~AM I AWAKE YET? ~

There are situations that no one would ever understand or imagine what it is like to go through on a daily basis. It is very difficult to sit back and watch your daughter hurt every day, knowing that no matter what you do, you cannot take that pain away. I am not only talking about visible pain but the pain that sits within one's self. Not all pain is visible, not all can be seen. I'm talking about the pain, torture, depression, anxiety and hatred for one's self. This is pain that they feel every day and no one can take that pain or feeling away, not even the individual. Yes, medicine may work but medicine cannot always repair your feelings deep inside but only repair your moods from crashing around like wild fire. Medicine may only stabilize that individual from acting on their feelings right away and make them think before they do. Medicine may only help the individual to deal with life day to day until it stops working, and then, what do you do? You either up the dose or try a new medicine and pray that it works. The sad part is the individual with the bipolar doesn't recognize when the medicine stops working; they believe that they are fine or okay. Without guidance, they are like a tornado or hurricane and spin out of control emotionally, mentally and physically. It's complete chaos. Not only does this affect their own life but also others that are around them, especially the loved ones that are the closest to them.

For me to sit back and watch the hurricane start it hurts me so deeply because I, as a mother, am supposed to keep my daughter safe, in control of her life and to always feel loved. It cannot always be done with the illness that she has. I try as a mother and best friend to make it known that I love her. I tell her every day that I love her more than anything in this world and that no matter what I always will and nothing will ever change the way I feel. I see the pain in her eyes and I hear the pain in her voice at times. I get replies such as, "No you don't! You hate me!" or "How can you love a freak?" This hurts me so deep inside, especially being that I am her mother and that she thinks that way, however I know it is not her fault. I can only hope that deep down inside that she realizes the love that I have her. Not only to hear the emotional pain that she is going through, but to also watch the physical pain that she puts herself through such as the cutting or scratching on herself. It hurts me so deep inside. Yes, you can tell the individual how you feel, however during their manic episodes they don't believe you. During their manic episodes, the individual believes that you don't love them, that you hate them. Yes, there are times I sit and cry because I can't take that pain away. There are times that I pray to God to please take that pain away from my little girl and to please give it to me so she can be happy again. I also ask "Why my daughter? Why my little girl?"

I have deeply thought about this hurricane not only in her life, but mine also and I have realized that this is not only a fight in our lives but also others out there. Maybe with me writing this I can help others out there and hopefully bring them to an understanding of bipolar and how to live with a loved one that has this illness. Help them realize that it is okay to cry, however don't blame yourself at all.

~ AWAKE! ~

Having a baby is a struggle within itself, especially when they don't want to sleep and stay awake all hours of the night. Maybe, just maybe you are lucky they sleep an hour for that day! Does anyone think anything of it since your baby is healthy? No, they don't. They just think it's the normal sleep routine or that they have their nights and days confused. So, what do you do? You, as a parent, figure that the doctors are right and just go with the flow.

The staying awake for hours on end persisted and when the child at the toddler stage finally becomes so exhausted that they crash and burn, you are so thankful! You are thankful that your child is asleep finally and that you can now rest peacefully and build up energy for the next hours that come your way.

Throughout the toddler stage the doctor will finally tell you just to give them a Melatonin and this will help your child sleep. So, hey you do that, however after a few months Melatonin becomes resistant. Their body is used to it and it doesn't faze them one bit. Now what? You, being a good parent and worried about your child, you take them back to the doctor. The doctor still says everything is well, healthy child and they will grow out of it.

Years go by and nothing changes and doctors still say this is normal that not everyone needs the same amount of sleep. What do you do once again? You live a normal life and do everything that you can and keep the same daily routine as much as possible. You do everything you possibly can to tire your child out so the household can get some sleep. This means that one parent is always awake so the other can function for the other children.

Being that well-educated parent that I am in the nursing field, I do research on sleeping and I myself, came up with nothing. I pulled out all of my college books and I absolutely found nothing, so I thought. Needless to say, not all of the symptoms were there at the time. Not being as young as she was. According to all of the research I had found at that time she just had issues with sleeping and being young, the research just stated that she would grow out of it. As a family, we just need to try to work on her schedule, do everything possible to make her tired, even if it meant that wherever she fell asleep you don't wake her, you let her there. If someone did wake her, this child was not going back to sleep, as you were in for it! As I remember if she was listening to music and dancing you let her alone. As you noticed that she was ready to fall over you took every cushion from the couch, every pillow and you barricaded her in with them so when she did fall, she had soft landing and that's where she slept. If not, she would be up for hours or the entire day with maybe one hour of sleep. Sounds exhausting, I know, and yes, it sure was!

~IMAGINATION~

We all know that when children are young they all have an imagination. They sit and play and talk to their imaginary friends or play with their imaginary pets. Having an imagination is known to be a healthy event for children as they grow and they learn from it. A child's imagination doesn't have any boundaries as they are young and learning from it. Their imagination is what helps them recognize what is real and what is not real. Children are able to develop, grow, and learn to become their own individual by having and using their imagination. As parents, we accept that and we also encourage the playtime right along with their imaginary friends or pets, whatever it may be.

When does, the imaginary play go too far? When does the imaginary play need to end? Having children, a parent is use to the imaginary play and doesn't think anything of it. We as parents play right along and keep encouraging it. Until you realize that your child really and I mean really believes that it is true or that they actually see what is imaginary to us but is really there in their own eyes.

I remember this so clearly, however did not think anything of it at the time because she was a child playing. I didn't really think too much of it until just recently. As my daughter was growing up she was like every other child out there and used her imagination. She had imaginary friends and even an imaginary dog. I use to play along and go with the flow until dad and I discussed one day that he actually thought that she believed her pet dog was real! I was in shock and even questioned it in my head a few times. I went over and over the situation in my mind for days. I sat back and watched her. She had a jump rope and she pulled it right along beside her every day in the house and all-day long. She would look at and say "I'm walking my dog." She would talk to it and when she went outside to play the jump rope came right along. She would say "My dog wants to go outside to play too." After watching her and analyzing the situation I told dad he was right. I mean she would even try to feed her dog and give the dog water. Back then I figured it's a jump rope. Make the jump rope disappear and then the imaginary dog would too. I took the jump rope and threw it in the trash, out of sight, out of mind, right? Nope not right away anyhow. She looked all over for that jump rope and I did not give in. I didn't have a clue what happened to that jump rope. She searched high and low for that jump rope for days! Finally, a word was not mentioned about it and I figured thank goodness, the end of the imaginary pet! Everything seemed well after that. Years went by and no mention of the imaginary dog. Imaginary in our eyes, however not really thinking it was real in her eyes. Who wants to believe that their child is seeing things that aren't really there at a such young age? We, as a family, pushed it into the back of our head and forgot about it. Like the situation never occurred.

~IS IT DEPRESSION? ~

Is it depression? How could I let my child become depressed and I never saw it coming? Why is it my child? Why does she have to take after me and end up with depression? Is she depressed or is it just a phase? These are the thoughts and feelings that race through your mind over and over again. Then there comes that denial stage, "No not my daughter. How could she be depressed? She has a family that loves her! She has a mom that shows her, and tells her every day. I give her hugs and kisses and nonstop I love you. What the heck?" Through that denial stage you keep the doors open to talk as you always have. You check on your child everyday asking is everything ok? Do you want to talk? Is there anything bothering? How do you feel?

As I first started seeing a difference in my daughter I noticed a change in her demeanor, the way she dressed and a difference in whom she hung out with. At first, I was blaming the social networks and took her away from all of them. I blamed the friends that she was hanging out with and started taking them away as much as I possibly could. I saw a difference in her with one individual she was hanging with and this the individual that first introduced my daughter into cutting. Yeah, you read that right...cutting! No, that is not cool at all! I was devastated when I first learned that my daughter was cutting. My heart hit the floor, my eyes filled with tears and I felt a huge emptiness in the pit of my stomach. No! why is she cutting? What the heck is wrong with her!? Is it me? Did I not pay enough attention to her and the cutting is the outcome? Who really wants to face the fact that their child is so depressed that they cut?

I sat back and looked at whom she was talking to and hanging out with. Yes, as parents, we confiscated her phone and researched every little piece of it, every app, and everything on social media. Read every text that came in and went out along with all phone calls. As I researched the phone I realized where the cutting from was coming from. Her newbie friend was a cutter! Oh, my thoughts were how did I not know? How did I not see this coming? How did I not know that she had a friend that was a cutter and as depressed as she was? In the phone messages and on wonderful social media my daughter stated that she was cutting her arms. When I first brought it to her attention that I knew, but not exactly how, she was denying it. She said someone else cut her. Even while she was outside playing she called me and said some boys were chasing her and cut her. Being the mom that I am I hunted these kids down and talked with the parents. I get home and look at her arms, sliced from the wrist to the almost the shoulder, I couldn't believe my eyes! I examined the cuts and you could tell they were self-inflicted. My heart hit the floor, my gut was filled with fear. My thoughts at this time is if a child has gone this far how much further will she go? Every time I brought the situation up she insisted that she didn't do it that these boys did it. My, my, my, what is a mother to do especially when you teach your child not to lie. I sort of dropped it and just kept the communication line open.

I am sure some of you are asking "Why don't you put your child into therapy or the hospital?"

My child was receiving therapy in a therapist's office and home-based therapy. Once a week, every week in the office and twice a week, three hour sessions each day at home. There wasn't much more therapy that I could get! Not to mention the therapist at the school helping as much as possible. What parent really wants to see their child in the hospital!? That is the last resort!

The depression that I noticed started in August 2015, however she seemed to feel better and acted really happy with everything. I figured she was okay. My daughter and I have always been really close and she always talked to me about anything. I loved that we were so close and open and tried to keep it that way. The trust was there and I figured she was telling me the truth and that she was happy.

As I started finding information on the social media sites that were talking about death, her dying and hating life so much I knew that the depression was not over. Now the bursts of sadness and self-mutilation was occurring more than I thought. The self-confidence was gone, crying more and more and the depression was back all of the time. She started telling me that she was not happy on the inside that she made herself look happy on the outside. She didn't want anyone to know how she was really feeling, putting up a front, like putting up a wall because she was ashamed and afraid. Fear was there, it was in her eyes just like the feeling of hopelessness and the feeling that everyone was against her and hated her.

~NIGHTMARE~

My nightmare started again when I thought it couldn't get any worse. I watched my daughter go through so many changes in just a small amount of time. I knew if her moods got worse I would have to admit her to the hospital. I never wanted to face this day, NEVER!

At this time, I had her in seeing a therapist at the school and also had two coming to the house which is called home based therapy. Her moods were swinging out of control to where she didn't want to talk to me, the one that was always there for her no matter what. She got to the point where she didn't want to talk to any of the therapist at all.

The day came where she was uncontrollable, not wanting to discuss anything at all, however you could see the depression in her eyes, the pain was there and I couldn't do anything to take it away, that was the worst part and worse feeling ever for a mom. The therapist was at the house trying to get her to sit down, be calm and talk. This was a mania day where she was talking so fast, talking about how everyone was against her and hated her. She put herself down and said she was no good, no one loved her and she packed her bag and said she was going to a friend's house to study. I knew she wasn't going to study, this is a very intelligent girl that doesn't need to study and still receives an "A". I told her if she left, I would call the cops and have her picked up. She didn't care, she left. My little girl whom always listens ignored what I just said and left with a packed bag. I knew this wasn't good. The therapist that was at the house said, "She is out of control, she's not stable, let's go get her." We drove up to her friend's house and she wouldn't come out. Her so called friend was not any help she wouldn't tell her to listen to her mom and come out. She was lying for her. The parent's in the house were no help neither, they wouldn't tell her you better listen to your mom. What kind of parents are they? I told her if she didn't come out that I would call the cops. Still no one was budging. I did what no parent ever wanted to do, called the cops on my daughter. I knew if I didn't the outcome was not going to be good, I just had the gut feeling. I made the decision and called the cops.

When the cops arrived, they talked to her and they were going to let her go. I sat in the back of the police car and told them that she's not okay, she's going to get hurt or hurt herself and I filled him in on everything that was going on. Guess the cop on duty didn't believe me and talked to the therapist and he told him the same thing and that she's not able to make decisions right now because she was not stable. The cop talked to me and said, "I see you care about your child and want the best for her. I will personally escort her to the hospital so they can evaluate her." Thank goodness, I'm getting some help! I was in tears all the way to the hospital and kept saying not my little girl. The denial stage hit and the guilty feeling inside because no one wants to do this to their own child.

Once at the hospital an evaluation was completed and they said she was not stable and needed admitted. By now her mania stage past and she realized what she did and agreed to stay at a hospital because she wanted the help. She knew something was wrong but had no idea what. Waited hours upon hours at the emergency room for them to find a psychiatric unit available. Around midnight they said, "Oh she can go home if she wants, she is stable now. "I said, "No I want to know what's going on before she hurts herself or someone else hurts her." She also agreed that she didn't want to go home that she wanted the help. Finally, at 5 am they find her a psychiatric unit close about, an hour away.

The hour drive was the longest drive ever. I was broken inside now. I knew what I had to do I just didn't want to face it. Got her in, admitted, she walked me to the door that I had to walk out of and leave her. I hugged her and told her I loved her and I would be there to see her every day. I hid the tears in front of her, being a brave mom. As I walked out the door and looked back at her, my heart hit the floor. I heard the door slam behind me, waiting on the elevator I cried so hard. Who would ever think that a mother would ever have to make this decision? I couldn't believe it was happening to me, to my daughter. I asked God, why? I had an hour drive back home, alone, and I was in tears the entire time. I was exhausted, hurt, and in denial of what was going on. I felt myself falling back into depression, but I knew I had to pull myself together. My other two kids needed me and my daughter still needed me more than ever now.

I caught myself being more and more depressed because my daughter wasn't home with me, I was missing her so much. I thought she would hate me now and that I was an awful mother. I caught myself just wanting to lay in bed and dwell on the situation until one day, I said to myself, "What are you doing? Why are you lying in bed? What good is laying in the bed going to help her?" I haven't mentioned, but I have a Bachelor and Master's degree in the healthcare field. I decided to get my butt out of the bed and do what I do best, research. I went to the library and borrowed every book imaginable on borderline personality, depression, schizophrenia and bipolar. I wasn't sure what I was dealing with however I figured it had to be more that depression. I started researching instead of lying in bed feeling sorry for myself and my daughter. She needed mom's help and I was going to do everything I possibly could. That's what mom's do!

~MISDIAGNOSED~

Hmmm, my daughter spent a week in the hospital and all they could come up with was depression and anxiety. I knew deep down inside there was more than depression and anxiety, but I couldn't prove it at this point. Then I figured maybe I was wrong, the doctors would know better. I accepted that diagnosis. I brought her home and everything seemed fantastic for a while, but I saw she still was not happy. I have depression, I knew it was more than that deep down inside. Mom's always know, they have that gut feeling. Without proof, what do you do? You accept it.

My daughter was home and we kept the therapy and made appointments to follow up with a psychiatric doctor. Everything was going great for a while. I figured I had my daughter back. I was happy. Until the cutting started again, the depressed moods and mood swings. It started again she thought everyone was watching her and hated her. All the doctors kept saying everything is fine. No, it wasn't! They weren't living under my roof! I knew something else was wrong. Through my research, I came up with a diagnosis of bipolar or schizoaffective disorder.

Everyone thought everything was fine, but she was back to not sleeping and packing her bags and wanting to leave. It was very difficult to live with because I never knew if I would wake up and she not be there or would she try to commit suicide. I was always worried, afraid, and living on edge. I tried staying awake when she was so I knew she would be okay. There was one night that I was awake until 4 am, I couldn't stay awake any longer I had to go to bed, I was beyond exhausted.

An hour later what do I wake up to? You will never guess! Unbelievable, the unthinkable and most scary ever! While I was sleeping along with everyone else in the household, my daughter had packed her clothes, put her medicine that she was taking for a diagnosis of anxiety and depression into the bag she was packing, took her dad's phone and reprogrammed it to be her phone by changing everything on it including the wallpaper and put a password on it. She then at some time started a fire on top of our dog's cage with the sheet that covered it and on a curtain, that covered our basement door to keep the cold air out. I never smelled the smoke or heard anything. Our dog woke her dad up barking and he went downstairs to catch her leaving the house and the smell of smoke. He found the curtains and sheets where on fire, thank goodness, they were flame retardant and went out on their own or the entire house would have gone up in smoke with the family. He asked her, "What are you doing? Where are you going?" She said, "Nowhere" At that time she was in a mania stage and didn't realize what she was doing. She came upstairs to me crying and said "I need help mom! Put me back in the hospital please." It's difficult to hear that coming from your own child. I just told her come lay with mom and get some sleep. She came and did just that and I held onto her the rest of the morning just cuddling with her and prayed that everything would be okay and that it would work out. Again, I'm fighting tears because I knew something else was wrong but the doctors where saying it's just depression. Even though she told them she was seeing things and hearing voices that were not there, it's just depression. No, I knew it wasn't depression but no one was helping me to get a better diagnosis.

~THE FIGHT BEGINS~

I fought with doctor's tooth and nail to get an MRI, magnetic resonance imaging, I knew that would tell us if there was an activity of schizophrenia or bipolar. Waiting was the hardest part besides getting a doctor to order it for me. I found the most awesome doctor to agree to order it and we went from there for a diagnosis. What actually helped with the diagnosis besides the MRI was the journal I kept. I was able to effectively communicate what the moods were, when they were and everything that occurred those days. That's the best thing I ever did was keep a detailed journal on a daily basis.

What I have learned from the journal was the symptoms, all the signs were there and I knew it but I needed more information to back my diagnosis up. One thing is to remember that each individual is different and they may vary over time. Each individual will have a different pattern, especially children compared to adults, some may be severe and some may not. Some individuals may become more depressed and others may have more hyperactivity. Children can go through episodes that cycle more rapidly than adults.

During mania, which is known as the manic phase the following may occur:

- Hyperactivity

- Creativity

- Euphoria

- Talking fast and difficult to understand

- Lack of sleep

- Feeling of being invincible/super human powers

When the individual is coming out of a mania episode the individual may go through the following:

- Reckless or risky behavior

- Anger

- Irritability

- Aggressive

- Pick fights with others for no apparent reason

- Delusional such hearing voices or seeing people/things that are not there

Symptoms that may persist:

- Feeling hopeless, empty inside and full of sadness

- Irritable and not knowing why

- Anxiety

- Sensitivity to light, smells, touch, loud noises

- Cannot find pleasure in anything at all like they use to at one time

- Fatigue not only physically but also mentally

- Change in appetite

- Sleep disturbance

- Inability to concentrate

- Wanting to die

Every day is a learning experience for me. I have researched bipolar disorders but living with it every day and watching a loved one go through it doesn't compare. You defiantly learn more with hands on experience. All the research in the world cannot equip you enough for the roller coaster ride in life.

To watch a loved one, specially your daughter, go through episodes of mania and all the feelings of hopelessness, depression, emptiness, risky behaviors, delusions such as hearing voices that were not there and seeing people that were not there along with the suicidal thoughts or tendencies is very difficult. You, yourself as a parent, start feeling depression, emptiness, hopelessness because you can't help the individual. I myself went through all those feelings, I was like a roller coaster too. I would sit and cry and say, "Why my little girl? Why me? Why couldn't God give this too me instead of her?" I didn't think I would make it through, I thought for sure I would lose my mind. I finally decided that I can't just sit back and watch this. I had to do something to help her and others. I then decided to take all of my knowledge, research, and my stories to put into this book to help others.

There were times that we would go out in public and the large groups or loud noises would set her into a mania. It took me a little while to figure it out, until she started hiding in restrooms to be alone. I would have to go after her and she would say, "I just want to hang out in here. I'm fine Mom, honest." She would be nervous, shaking, and distant, defiantly wasn't her. Finally, she would start telling me, "I just want to leave, there's too many people." I completely understood, I deal with anxiety so I could appreciate her honesty and we started working through it slowly.

It is very difficult to find a doctor that will diagnose bipolar at a young age. Doctors despise diagnosing young, most want to wait until they are 18 or over. As I said we need to control it now, not later, not when it's too late. The disorder needs treated as soon as possible not only for the patient but also for the family and friends' due to safety concerns that can occur.

~THE DIAGNOSIS~

As not only a professional in the field of healthcare, but also as a mother I knew something was wrong. I just knew deep down inside that she didn't have just depression or anxiety. Yes, depression was there, anxiety was there, but I knew there was something more, but I couldn't put my finger on it at that time. I suffer from depression and anxiety myself so I knew what that was like. I just knew there was more, but my issue was finding the right doctor, the right tests to be done.   You have an idea at that time what it is, either schizophrenia, bipolar, or schizoaffective disorder, which is schizophrenia and bipolar. You know from your own research, your own background and study in the medical field. You also know from the genetic background that runs in the family, however you also know that the doctors don't want to diagnose it neither at a young age. In order to get the individual, the right help, you need that diagnosis to get the correct medicine that is needed and therapy. Something must be done as your child spirals out of control! There must be something to bring your child back so they don't hurt themselves or hurt someone else.

You see the difference in your child that no one else may see. You know your child better than anyone else. You see your child hurt, the tears, the depression, the anxiety, the emotional pain, physical pain that they may be inflicting upon themselves. You see the rage, the mood swings, the mania of not sleeping, the fast talking, not eating, not bathing, the communication that you once had is gone and even at the times the fear in their eyes because they feel hated or hatred towards others. They feel as though everyone is watching them, hates them and is talking about them. The scary part is they may even see this happening even though it actually isn't, it's a delusion that seems so real to them. They may even see a loved one that they are closest to hurting them, physically, emotionally or mentally even when it actually hasn't happened, but in their mind it actually has. They even see someone following them all the time, watching them even if it hasn't happened, but to them it has. This part is difficult for someone to understand if they have not been through this. You may just say that they are crazy, but they are not.

You will see the possessions that they once enjoyed, they no longer find joy in them at all. The ability to feel pleasure is gone, as if they are numb.

The individual doesn't realize all of this happening, they feel normal as you and I. They feel fine except for the depression and emptiness.

Certain stresses in their life will not only cause anxiety, but the mood disturbances and the risky behaviors. They may not be able to handle a lot of noise, people, and may even want to hide or leave to isolate themselves.

I will never forget the family went to a church event where a band was playing outside. Yes, a lot of people where there, however the function was outside. You would think that would be fantastic, lots of room and not closed in. Nope, it wasn't. There were still too many people, too much noise, and I'm sure a lot of confusion for my daughter. She said she was heading to the restroom and I said okay. I noticed she was gone for 15 minutes. I went to check on her and got her back outside with the family. Five minutes later she is back in the restroom for another 10 minutes. I went to go get her and she's sitting in a corner alone on her phone and finally telling me she wanted to leave that she didn't feel well. I asked her if it was because it was crowded and she said yes. At this time, she had an entire different personality such as nervousness, upset, almost in tears, depressed, and she felt closed in entirely and just wanted to leave. I did what any mother would, said ok let's go home. I gave her a hug, told her I loved her and appreciated her telling me she wanted to leave. I try, and always, will keep the communication open between my daughter and I.

~BIPOLAR, WHAT IS IT? ~

Bipolar relates to mood disorders in which not only the depressive episodes occur but also the manic or hypomanic episodes occur.

As I mentioned earlier in the last chapter that the symptoms of bipolar are the following:

- Feeling superiority

- Rapid speech

- Impulsive behavior

- Living on the edge, risky behavior

- Hazard to themselves and or others

- Insomnia

- Believing in things that are not there or not true.

- An imaginary world, life they believe in however it doesn't exist, it's just not there.

The sad part is that the individual doesn't realize when they are entering this stage. The individual feels normal as if nothing can bring them down and there's no stopping them. They feel self-confident, beautiful, smart, life can't get any better at this time until that low comes. As that low comes, watch out everyone! When the low hits, the individual is very irritable, has self-doubt with in themselves, they feel ugly, self-confidence is gone. The individual is depressed, feelings of hopelessness, alone, suicidal and they are destructible. They even have hate not just for themselves but also everyone else's around them, especially when they are told "No!"

When the individual is in the depressive stage they lose their energy, become exhausted and the joy in their life is no longer there that they may have had an hour ago. The individual feels depressed at all times and they feel that that there isn't any hope for their life. The individual is as negative as negative can get! During this period is when they are suicidal and may feel just so low that they may even attempt it at this time, because they feel that they are worthless and have nothing to live for anymore.

Manic attacks in children can last for days and even as long as months. When children go through mania, unless you know the child and learn about bipolar disorder you won't even realize it right away. During this phase, the child becomes irritable and hyperactivity occurs.

Children can also bounce back and forth from the depressive state to the mania state several times throughout a day and this is what is called a mixed state. Being that it is just a child having these episodes, as they get older they can have more and more occurring on a regular basis throughout their life.

~ BIPOLAR BRAIN~

Doctors really don't know the causes of bipolar, however it is medically known how the chemicals in the brain react and which chemicals are linked to each feeling within the body. The chemicals in the brain are norepinephrine, serotonin and dopamine.

Norepinephrine is a chemical in the brain that is released when it responses to a stress. The norepinephrine is classified as a neurotransmitter and the chemical is released from the neurons which affects the organs of the body. Norepinephrine is also known as a stress hormone.

Serotonin is the chemical that takes care of the body functions such as sleep, being awake, eating, everyday impulses, learning and memory. Serotonin is also linked to the mood disorders.

Dopamine regulates the pleasure feeling and emotional reward feelings.

~TESTING FOR A DIAGNOSIS~

The first step is making an appointment with a doctor that specializes with the bipolar disorder along with a psychiatrist. You are going to need them both anyways so make both appointments as soon as you have a suspicion that the disorder may exist.

You and the child will meet with the doctor where an evaluation will occur. The evaluation will include the following:

Physical Examination which will include lab tests to see if there are any medical issues that could be causing any symptoms that your child may be having.

Psychiatric Evaluation: This is why I said to make an appointment with a psychiatrist ahead of time right along with the doctor. With the psychiatrist, an evaluation will be completed where they will ask questions about the child's thoughts, feelings and their behavior.

Mood/Behavior Chart: In other words, keep a daily journal which is going to help with the diagnosis. When writing in your journal make sure you are detailed every day specially when outbursts, mood swings, irritability, feelings or sleep patterns are involved. Write it all down. When in doubt write it down. This will help you in the long run. I've learned from experience, trust me.

Following the Criteria for Bipolar: Once the evaluation is completed, then the psychiatrist will compare the individual's symptoms with the criteria for bipolar. The psychiatrist will also compare the symptoms to other related disorders based from the Diagnostic and Statistical Manual of Mental Disorders, also known as the DSM-V.

Everything sounds so easy, right? Nope!

Here's one issue with diagnosing children, their symptoms vary and change faster than adults. Children can go through cycles of mania so much faster than an adult and they are more difficult to catch unless you are looking for the disorder. At times, a child may be diagnosed improperly such as ADHD, depression, or behavior disorders such as an occupational defiant disorder. Even though the individual is diagnosed, watch your child and do your research. Research every disorder if needed so you are aware. I know, I spent hours in the library and months researching nonstop!

~MRI OR CAT SCAN FOR BIPOLAR~

Even though an MRI can show deformities in the brain that suggests there is an underlying issue, the doctors do not rely on it at this time for a diagnosis of bipolar, however the scan will show if there are other neurological diseases that may be an underlying issue.

~TYPES OF BIPOLAR~

Bipolar 1: The individual has at least one manic or mixed episode. With bipolar 1 the individual will have one or more episodes and they experience a hypomanic stage before a full mania. Bipolar 1 can also include psychosis during the mood disorder. Most with bipolar 1 suffer with depression and then the stage cycles between mania and depression. The good news is those with bipolar 1 can live a normal life.

Bipolar 2: This is similar to bipolar 1. The moods cycle between the highs and lows overtime.

The high mood never reaches full blown mania. This disorder is less intense when it comes to the elevated moods and they are hypomanic episodes.

Individuals with bipolar 2 have had at least one hypomanic episode in their life and most suffer from depression. These individuals can also live a normal life.

Bipolar NOS: This diagnosis is not otherwise specified, which means it doesn't fall under any category with in the established sub types. The individual may have symptoms however does not meet the requirement for a diagnosis of bipolar 1 or bipolar 2.

~SYMPTOMS~

The symptoms start with a depressive disorder can lead to irritability and anxiety. The manic episode in children is a hyperactivity right along with irritability and mood swings that can start from mild to severe. Nervousness follows and then the rapid speech begins and you can't understand them. The individual may even seem as if they are a different person all together. At that time of when they are in a mania they may seem like they know what they are doing and not even realize they are going through a mania. In reality, they have no clue of what they are doing or saying at that time. They are in their own world, not ours, it all seems so real to them. Heck, they may even see things or people that are not there and see things happening that actually in reality are not, but it seems so real to them.

Some of the signs that are listed you will notice, however some you may not catch right away such as:

- Not being able to pay attention or to sit still

- Having difficulty staying organized

- Hyperactivity at times to where the individual seems to have so much energy that they are restless and just cannot sit still no matter what

- Problems with starting tasks and completing them

- The individual seems so exhausted that all they want to do is sleep for days or they just don't have any motivation at all. They won't talk and they close that communication channel completely off.

MOODS

When the moods come, just beware, because they can be strong! Sometimes your best bet is to back away sometimes and just sit back and watch for safety. The moods can be as follows:

The individual can have feelings have sadness for no reason at all and no matter what you do just isn't enough for them.

Irritability can come at any giving time on and off or the entire day. Irritability can occur over the simplest things like their hair isn't sitting just right or their makeup isn't perfect.

The individual always feels that they are not good enough.

The individual just isn't happy with anything that day, everything is just awful no matter what it is.

The moods can be so explosive with the screaming at family members for the simplest little noises and then all of a sudden, she calms down as if nothing ever happened. I would just want to ask at that point who are you and is everything ok?

Eventually at some point you will see the individuals sleep pattern change. You notice the individual will possibly be awake for days or sleep one hour and be awake the rest of the day. You're just sitting back saying to yourself "Where do you get this energy? I really need it!" When the highs in mania occur, they don't need any sleep, they are on their high! A high we all wish we had at times.

Along with the mood swings, change in sleep, the individuals eating habits will also change. Some individual's may not eat at all while others will eat excessively, especially on carbohydrates and foods high in sugar.

The individual's interest will change. Activities they once enjoyed and took pride in, they no longer care about anymore. Seems as though when the mania takes over they, don't enjoy anything anymore.

Not only do their interests change but also their friendships. If they once had friends, close friends, guarantee they will no longer have them. One reason why is no one understands what that individual with bipolar is going through and they don't care to understand. Especially at a young age because most parents don't sit with their children and explain illnesses with them or teach them that everyone is different, no one is the same. It seems as soon as the individual makes a friend, they become annoyed with them quick and don't want bothered and that is because they want left alone. They don't always want company or want to hear someone talking nonstop. They are happy being alone and staying with their own routine.

What I have spoken about is not even the worse part of all. The worse is yet to come!

Along with all of the mentioned changes in the individual, there is a dark side to all of this. With everything changing and they don't know why, of course they have an emptiness inside, however they are unaware why at that time. With the emptiness, comes loneliness, sadness, fear, rage, depression, and anxiety. Well, they don't know how to cope with all of these emotions and change at one time. How can they cope? This is where they turn to the only thing they know, understand, and believe will end all of the pain, suicide. This is where suicidal ideations and tendencies occur. The individual actually wants to die just to take the pain all away and then self-mutilation occurs.

According to the CDC (Centers for Disease Control and Prevention) in 2004, suicide was the highest cause of death amongst all age groups. Individuals aged 14-64, was right with that ranking.

Regarding suicide in the United States, 32,439 individuals committed suicide, crazy right! That is an awfully high rate, I thought it was unbelievable. I never in million years thought I would ever see that huge number.

Believe it or not women are three times more likely to attempt suicide than men, however men are four times more likely to complete suicide.

Regarding the individuals having a history of bipolar, 100% of them have attempted suicide at some point in time in their lives.

BEHAVIOR

Violent rages come and go for no reason what so ever and the individual may be aware that it is happening but don't know why. They can't always control their moods, for anyone to live this way everyday would be awful. I couldn't imagine feeling a rage and not knowing or understanding why, specially a child. Poor judgment is another side effect that they have, that's not mentioning when a mania is occurring. When mania is occurring, they live off of impulses completely without any thought put into their actions and consequences that they must deal with afterwards.

Beware when the individual doesn't get their own way. In most children, the outrage would be considered a tantrum, however this is much worse. Doors slamming, items being thrown, stomping, screaming, any type of backlash. I have heard so many times how hated I was, pacing back and forth because they don't know what to do with the energy inside of them.

DISORDERS THAT COME WITH BIPOLAR

Anyone can have any of the following disorders, however individuals with bipolar are more likely to suffer from one or all of the following such as panic disorder and obsessive-compulsive disorder at some point of time, whether it's recognized right away or not. Post-traumatic stress disorder is another one, along with social phobia and the main disorder is depression along with anxiety. Let's discuss the disorders that I have not yet reviewed, in the following sections.

ANXIETY

Anxiety is automatic with bipolar due to all the worries about their illness that they now have to live with. That's not even mentioning their basic everyday life, along with worrying about being judged by everyone or is everyone looking at them, which is how they feel most of the time.

The anxiety can become so high to where the individual will hide in a bathroom until everyone leaves. While they are out in a crowd with a lot of people they look through everything and only see tunnel vision and only look and concentrate on what makes them feel safe. One thing my daughter found to really help her is to have her phone on her, put head phones in even if there isn't any music on. By using the headphones this seems to block out that extra noise for her to where she can feel comfortable going out.

Another sign are constant complaints about always hurting such as complaining of headaches, muscle aches, and possible broken bones that do not exist.

Due to the anxiety, their sleep becomes disrupted and unregular sleep patterns begin.

∞

~SOCIAL SKILLS~

Think about how your child is doing socially. How are they during social events? Is he/she interacting with other children or are they sitting on the side line? Do they have any friends at all?

What I noticed is my daughter had stopped socializing with other children and was sitting on the sidelines when I took her to special events such as church outings. When being at special events she would hide from the situation and try to leave early. For instance, telling me she didn't feel well and became withdrawn and depressed. Friends she once had where no longer friends. She started choosing friends that had other issues that I didn't agree on her hanging out with them, friends she normally would not choose.

I also noticed that when the household had to change routines, she was not the same person. Her moods would change and she was very withdrawn, however it took me awhile to notice this.

The strange part is even though she hated socializing in huge crowds there were times she was overly friendly and giving out too much information about herself without knowing anything about the individual. Hmm, yes that was part of a mania that I was unaware of at the time. Wish I would have known.

~OUT OF PLACE THOUGHTS~

Thoughts that are out of place are another sign and unless you have a close relationship where you allow your children to tell you anything at all, an open line of communication, you may not even realize this is going on.

Hallucinations may occur where the individual is seeing other people that are not there and the hallucination may follow them and tell them what to do. They may feel threatened from the hallucination thinking that it might hurt them or other family members.

Thoughts that are out in left field that makes no sense to anyone else, makes sense to them, rambling thoughts that are not in order.

They may not trust anyone; the trust just isn't there at all. The trust may even be broken with the one individual that is the closest to them that they love the most of all. They feel that no one loves them, no one cares, and that everyone is out to get them, even though it's not true. They believe it is the truth. If you are a parent going through this, be patient, as the love will come back and so will the trust. Just be there for them no matter what, no matter how many times you hear, "I hate you." "You don't love me" no matter how many times they push you away when you hug them. Keep

43

those hugs coming and eventually it will subside and you will receive the love back.

Frustration is a huge ordeal because their thought process is not always up to speed. They know what they want to say but may have a difficult time wording it properly. Concentration is not their best forte, they have a difficulty concentrating, especially when there's so much activity going on. Sensory overload occurs while there's too much activity going on and they can't handle it. They will shut down, become depressive and withdraw from the entire situation. You've got to handle this situation with care so they don't go into a manic phase.

~CHAOS~

Does their complete life seem like complete chaos, disorganized and everything in shambles? Oh, yes, this is another sign. My daughter use to be so organized, her room cleaned, school papers all organized, and clothes all hung up. Hmm, now it's completely different. In fact, I am not sure how she finds anything in her room. The bedroom is in complete disarray! Clothes on the floor, hangers on the floor, papers not in any type of order, as if a tornado came through. If this is the only sign that there is then I can live with it. We will work on that together and eventually she will be back in order.

~OBSESSION~

There may be certain role models that they are obsessed about, certain readings that they obsess over or different writings that they will read over and over and over again. You can obsess about it yourself and agitate even more and nag them about it or you can try to redirect their thoughts. Eventually the obsession will end. I know, I nagged and nagged and worried nonstop about it until I figured it's time for me to stop because I am making it worse. I just listened to whatever the obsession was about, talked about it and eventually it ended.

Obsession may occur with every day routines or how certain things have to be in order. Look at their routines from day to day. Are they keeping the same routine and you don't even realize it? Certain steps they do every morning when they wake up or do before they go to bed? Throwing that routine off can upset them and ruin their entire day! Breaking their routine can cause frustration, confusion and anxiety which will build up and cause them to lash out, shut down or make them become withdrawn. Something so simple as a routine, that we ourselves don't think about and take for granted, not realizing that when we break their routine up what it does for them.

~IN SEARCH OF A DOCTOR~

Something that sounds so simple, finding a doctor. Yes, sounds simple, however it is not. I went through many doctors until I found one that actually cared enough to not only listen to me, but to also listen to her. To my surprise, I found many doctors that wouldn't listen to children. An adult can tell the doctor what they see and hear but cannot tell exactly what the child is feeling. The doctor needs both to properly evaluate. I went through my share of doctors and the way they want to evaluate, I was really fed up and wasn't sure what else to do. I knew the diagnosis that was given to us was wrong. I knew there was more than just depression and anxiety. I just wasn't sure if it was schizophrenia or bipolar or both. I needed to rule out schizophrenia, at least I was hoping to rule it out. See what was helping me is that I have a background in the medical field, I studied psychology. I had done my homework and researched different mental illnesses and so did my daughter. She knew there was something more than depression and anxiety herself. She was in the spot I was, debating on the schizophrenia or bipolar. My daughter went to the library and checked out the same books I did and read up on mental illnesses also. A 9-year-old researching for an answer on a mental illness, yes, she knew something else was wrong.

Finally got a doctor to sit with her, complete evaluations, listened to her and myself. The doctor listened to me and ordered an MRI (magnetic resonance imaging) so we could hopefully rule out schizophrenia.

The fight of finding the right doctor was finished, now it was time to fight with the insurance company because they didn't think it was necessary to complete the MRI. Really! Not necessary! What part doesn't make it necessary? The part that she was in a hospital for a week? The part that she was diagnosed with depression and anxiety, which is wrong? The part that she's self-mutilating herself? The part that she is hallucinating? The part that she kept trying to run away and not sure why? Maybe the part that she tried to burn the house down with everyone sleeping! I couldn't seem to understand what part didn't they understand. What part didn't make it important or necessary enough to run the tests that not only I asked for but the doctor also requested? I tell you what. I fought with the insurance company and I threatened to go to their office and pull them over the counter! I threatened them with the news media. I shouldn't have to do that, that's why we pay for insurance, to cover for whatever is needed. To me this was an emergency because I knew if she was not put on the proper medicine and had the proper therapy it was just going to get worse. I knew I was also looking at the possibility of losing my daughter forever. I was not letting that happen!!!!

~DIAGNOSIS/MISDIAGNOSIS~

Let me tell you, I went through so much that I was ready to just give up. I was lost with not knowing what to do, not knowing what I was dealing with but I knew something had to be done. There were times all I would do was sit down and cry. I was losing my mind. I saw every day that my little girl was hurting and I couldn't do anything to help her. Mom couldn't do anything to help her. As a parent, we do whatever is needed. Absolutely anything for our children. I was at my wits end, exhausted from staying up nights upon nights on end to make sure she was safe. Making sure that the entire family was safe.

I mentioned earlier that she was in the hospital for a week and all they could say she was diagnosed with depression and anxiety. They put her on medicine and she seemed to be fine for a few weeks until disaster struck again. I dug into all their paperwork and my paperwork said exactly what I mentioned. The home-based therapy paperwork from the exact same hospital said it was only anxiety. The doctor I had couldn't even get the paperwork. Really? What the heck is going on?

Never go with one diagnosis, no matter whom it is. Their huge mistake, not knowing what they were doing caused my daughter to become worse and someone else could have gotten hurt or she could have really hurt herself.

Thank goodness, I looked more into everything and really completed my research. I should have done it earlier, but I, myself, wasn't in the right state of mind neither. I had to pull myself together and it took all I could do to do that. I thought I was going to be the next one in the hospital. I knew my daughter needed me and no one else was there to advocate for her. I also had two other children that needed me and I had to keep myself together. I couldn't lose my mind, not yet, anyways.

~HELPING YOUR CHILD COPE~

Once you have the proper diagnosis, now it's time for you to cope and to help your child cope. It's not easy, it's going to be rough not only for the child but also for you. Even though you're having a difficult time with the diagnosis you can't let your child see that. You have to hide your feelings and be the strong one. Your child needs you more than anything right now.

Depending on the age of the child and how mature they are, each child is different. I was lucky in a way because my daughter may have only been 10 as of now, however she was more mature for her age. I basically talked to her like an adult. What really did help is my daughter and I have always been close and I kept the communication line open. I have always wanted to know what my children are thinking, what they are doing in their life even if it's something I didn't want to hear, I still listened. Heck, I still do and always will. Another thing that helped is she is like me and researches everything. She knew something was wrong but wasn't sure what it was and she didn't want to tell me right away because she thought I would think she was crazy. I assured her I would never ever think that. Never! I told her everyone has their issues, they just deal with it and learn to live with whatever it is. Many times, I heard and still hear how she thinks she is a freak. I have always told her if she's a freak so am I because I live with depression, so I guess I am a freak too. She has now learned to accept what she has and understands that she will always need medicine and therapy to live a normal life. I explained to her that it's just like having diabetes. The individual that has diabetes needs medicine to live and so do you. Nothing is different. To this day there are difficult times but I remain here and open to always discuss it with her. The key is *COMMUNICATION* with your child. In fact, I am so proud of her because she wants to help other children that have psychological disorders and tell her story. She wants to become an advocate and I stand behind her all the way. She will be the best advocate out there because she has firsthand knowledge, she has been through it and understands it.

~HOW CAN YOU COPE AS A PARENT? ~

Dealing with your loved one or child being diagnosed with bipolar, or any other disorder, or disease, is so much like the stages of dying. It is in fact the same stages. I know I went through every single one of them.

Let's go through the stages together and explain what exactly they are. The following stages of dying are based on Kubler-Ross's Model. As I was going through everything with my daughter this is what I first thought of, it was just as if she died. She didn't, but a part of her did, there was a drastic change and I felt like I lost her forever.

The first stage is Denial. This is where the individual says "No, not me. Not my daughter, not my child." This is a defense mechanism that helps ease the individual's anxiety and helps them deal with the underlying issues.

Anger is the second stage which is where acceptance has taken place and fueled with anger, rage and resentment. The resentment can be directed towards others, especially those that are close to them.

Bargaining is the third stage and this may happen with family, friends and even God. I did ask God to please take it all away from my daughter and give it to me. I asked why her every day for the longest time. When I see her going through a difficult time I still ask why. At times, you may come back to this stage or others.

Depression is the fourth stage and the individual may sink into a deep depressed state or they may figure that they have already lost and give up.

Acceptance is the last stage where the individual has found peace and they are calm. Individuals are able to reflect and embrace the battle. Accept what it is and let's find ways to work with it, deal it and make it the best that we can to live our lives to the fullest that we can and find all the happiness that there is.

~WHAT WOKE THE BEAST? ~

What is bipolar and where does it come from? What awakens the bipolar from within the individual and causes the chaos in their lives that they once never had? We do know from research that bipolar is a partially genetic and stress related disorder.

According to all of the research I have conducted no one is guaranteeing that bipolar disorder is genetically caused, however families with the background of bipolar somewhere in the family have an increase and risk for not only bipolar but also schizophrenia or schizophrenia effective disorder. What this suggests is that this is only a partially shared gene for these disorders. Research is still being conducted on the genes and the gene mutations.

Stress can also be a huge factor with bipolar disorder. The individual can have the gene within them and it may not be completely mutated, however the stressors in their life can be too much for them to handle which causes the bipolar to erupt from within.

Stress can be very harmful on an individual, not only on their body but also psychologically and emotionally. Each individual can handle a different type of stress and some can handle more than others. Stress can impact each individual differently such as some individuals may gain weight, some may lose weight and others just get to the point that they cannot take it anymore and may have a nervous breakdown. There are others that the stress may cause bipolar to mutate which will cause manias. Stress in an individual's life that has bipolar can cause the mania to erupt and therefor causing the manic-depressive disorder to set in.

Major stresses could be caused from a variety of situations such as a new birth in the family, a death in the family, relationships in the family not working out and even bullying that occurs in and out of the school systems.

~ HOW IS YOUR CHILD COPING WITH BIPOLAR DISORDER? ~

Individuals with bipolar disorder, it isn't uncommon for them at all to suffer from depression at some point in their life. The depression that they may have could last from only a few hours to a few days, maybe a few weeks and possibly even longer, depending on the individual and the stressors in their life. Each individual is different and so is each situation that they are in that may be causing the depressive mood. However, throughout my researching period I have found that is has been founded that women with bipolar disorder may have more depressive episodes than what men do.

Those diagnosed with bipolar are also known to attempt or complete suicide. Throughout my research, I have found that individuals with bipolar, that there is as many as one in five patients that actually complete suicide. This isn't just attempting it, but actually completing it.

Another way an individual may choose to cope is through drugs or alcohol. Individuals with bipolar disorder choose to medicate with drugs or alcohol because they want to try to numb the symptoms that they deal with on a daily basis. The symptoms that they are trying to medicate are anxiety, depression and the pain that they feel inside of one's self. All of these feelings may become so overwhelming that they turn to drugs or alcohol just to get rid of the discomfort that they are feeling. They don't realize that turning to the drugs or alcohol is going to trigger the depression or manic episodes.

I have found that 56% of individuals that had experimented with drugs or alcohol, that 46% of them had abused them and 41% ended up addicted to drugs or alcohol. Believe it or not alcohol was the most common abused substance.

Believe it or not substance abuse is actually more common in young males compared to older males or females. Younger men seem to be the riskiest and the most self-destructive.

There is logic behind all of this madness. The reasoning behind all of the drug or alcohol addiction has to do with the brain chemistry of an individual with bipolar. Those that are diagnosed with bipolar have an abnormal level of serotonin, dopamine and norepinephrine, which is what we discussed in an earlier section. Well, these chemicals affect the appetite, metabolism, sleep and the body's ability to handle stress. What most individuals don't understand is these chemicals also affect the moods and the emotions of the individual. The use of drugs and alcohol interferes with the way the individuals brain processes all the chemicals from within in, and this is what causes emotional instability, depression, and mood swings.

~STEPS TO TAKE WITH YOUR CHILD ~

Since you now have a diagnosis, it's time to take some steps with your child together. No matter what age he or she is it's time to support him/her all the way, through the good and bad, through the rough and smooth. Just hold on tight because it will be a roller coaster ride!

Now that you have a diagnosis it is time to accept it. This is the first phase, accepting and then you can move on once the denial is gone.

The second step is finding a psychiatrist if you have not already done so and keeping all your appointments with them. As long as they have been diagnosed with bipolar, yes, a psychiatrist is needed and will always be needed. Don't ever stop! This gives the child time to vent and discuss issues that may arise that maybe they don't want to discuss with you completely, only because you are the parent. Even if they have discussed the issue with you, maybe it helps to have that extra ear to just listen. There is no such thing as having too many individuals involved. One day you may need the psychiatrist too back your child up in school for extra help, you just never know.

Medicine is the third step and can be the difficult step. It's difficult seeing your child take medicine every day, however if it helps them to live their life, I say go for it when it's needed. Unfortunately, with bipolar it is needed before the disorder progresses to become worse and they have no idea what is reality or fake. Eventually they won't be able to tell because the disease will progress. Help your child now, not later when it's too late. If one medicine doesn't work, doesn't mean another won't. Sometimes it's a hit or miss game unfortunately. That's why you find a good doctor that you trust that has been working with this disorder for years. While your child is on the medicine, yes, keep a close eye on them on how the medicine is reacting to them and how they are acting at all times. Keep a journal so you don't forget pertinent information for your next appointment. Everything is important, the way they are acting, feeling, what they are doing, sleeping patterns, everything!

When I was first going through all of this, yes, it was very difficult. I was in tears every day, sometimes off and on throughout the day. I couldn't take it, I had no one to help me through this that really understood anything. My so-called friends were not friends anymore and all they thought was my daughter was crazy. They didn't want to have anything to do with myself or her. Shame on them for being so ignorant! They know who they are if they ever read this book. My daughter was going through enough and so was I having to worry about individuals that didn't matter to us. I had to deal with my daughter feeling awful about herself at this time and we still go through it, so it actually never goes away. Her feelings about herself back then and now is the following:

- She's different. Well tell me whom isn't!?

- She's a freak. I always hated this one and still do. She is not a freak, she is whom she chooses weather others like it or not.

- She's no good. Oh, yes, she is! She is awesome, intelligent, beautiful, kind hearted and much more.

- She is sad, angry, depressed and frustrated. Yes, she is at times and it gets better because at one time she was so much worse. With medicine give it a good six months to find your child again within themselves. They will come back out, but you have to be there the entire way and show them love.

- She worries about ending up in a hospital again. Well, who wouldn't? I sure would! As long as mom is around, I won't let that happen unless it is needed. No worries there.

~YOUR CHILD NEEDS YOU AS THEIR ADVOCATE~

If you are not willing to stick beside your child through the roller coaster ride of highs and lows, good times and bad times, then it is time for you to back away and find someone that is. Your child needs an advocate right now, someone that will stand behind them all the way and decide what medicine is working and isn't. Not only has your child's life changed so has yours. You will always have to be there for them no matter what. You no longer have a life of your own. You will be lucky to be able to hold onto a full-time job when episodes occur at school and you are always getting phone calls or have to pick them up because they had a bad day and it isn't going well for them. If you don't pick them up, then there's a chance they will go through a mania and you will be picking them up later that day whether you want to or not.

Now you are not only a mom or dad, now you are their advocate. They need someone to stand behind them and fight for them. They need someone they trust to make sure they are receiving all of the care they need and that they are getting all of the help that they should be getting. The help is not only from the doctors, but also from the school for everything that they possibly can qualify for. You may be told that your child doesn't qualify for an IEP. If so you need to do the research and find a way to get your child help. They are disabled now and do qualify even if the school wants to turn them down, find a niche to get them help, because believe me there is one, you just have to find it.

The fight in the school system may begin with the child's teacher and they may turn you down saying they are not disabled or don't qualify because their grades are so good in all areas but one. Take your steps up the ladder of the school, don't give up, fight and research!

~INSURANCE, WHY HAVE IT? ~

The insurance that you pay into every paycheck, what do you think they should do to help with bipolar disorder? Hmmm, I pay into it, maybe they should cover all that is necessary, right? No questions asked when a serious diagnosis comes up...take care of it! However, they don't do that. I am supposed to have the best insurance, however sometimes I don't think so. I had a doctor order an MRI so we could rule out schizophrenia and the insurance wasn't sure if that was necessary. Really? People could be getting hurt and they don't think it's necessary. Well I do. Obviously, something is wrong and we need a diagnosis. Yes, it is necessary to start testing and start ruling diagnosis out to see what we come up with. Unfortunately, it's the only way to do it. I had to call right along with the doctor and staff and write why we felt it was necessary. The insurance sure doesn't look at their paperwork, do they? If so they would have seen why I wanted it. Hmm, bipolar, schizophrenia, schizophrenia effect, borderline....... yes, we needed the testing to see what all we possibly could be dealing with. This was affecting my life, the family's life and most of all my daughter's life. She couldn't function on the daily basis and something needed done before I lost my little girl, my only little girl that was once happy.

~FINDING A DOCTOR THAT FITS YOUR CHILD'S NEEDS~

It is difficult to find a good doctor period. Most doctor's now, won't spend time with their patient to get to know them. It's hard to find a doctor to listen to a child! I got very lucky when I found the doctor that I did. She is fantastic, listens not only what I have to say but also to what my daughter has to say and watches her body language during our meetings. What the children have to say is very important because the care is for them. Without their input then it's a guessing game. When looking for a doctor and knowing that they are a proper fit for the family you want to look for the following:

- The most important, is does your child get along with the doctor?

- Does your child trust that doctor and is he or she open to them about their feelings?

- Does the doctor take their time and listen to not only the parent but also the child? (no matter how long it takes for the child to explain what's going on)

~ACCEPTING THE DIAGNOSIS~

The most difficult to do is to get your child to accept the diagnosis that they now have. The disorder that they must now live with, acknowledge it and become friends with it, not fight it. The child must acknowledge their diagnosis and learn to live with it.

Recognizing the changes in the moods are another sign that they must learn to look for. They need to recognize when their moods are switching nonstop so they can learn how to control them or understand what to do when they start becoming out of hand.

Dealing with their moods is only one separate issue but they must learn how they respond to it properly. They must learn how to cope with these shifts that they are not use to.

Oppositional behavior is one of the main disorders with bipolar and can be very difficult to handle. This is a defiant disorder that you as a parent must recognize along with the child. No matter what you say you are wrong and don't know anything. Therapy will help not only you but also the child on how to deal with their behaviors in certain situations.

No matter what your child has you must build independence. They must be able to take care of their daily activities such as grooming, bathing, dressing, brushing their teeth, brushing their hair, and feeding themselves. They must be able to go into a public facility and be able to cope on their own with anxiety, depression, etc. and be able to function without you by their side.

Therapy can help you and your child with social skills of going out into public and dealing with others, along with organizational skills such as organizing their life and being able to cope on their own with keeping a tidy room and being able to find items that they need.

Another difficult pattern that there is going to be to break is the negative thoughts that they have at all times and their negative behavior. Remember their self-confidence is down and so is their self-esteem. All of these needs rebuilt again.

Impulsivity can be another huge step to overcome because their entire life they have built on impulsiveness and that's what they are used to. This is a big change for them to stop and think of consequences that may occur due to their actions.

67

~KEEP A JOURNAL ON THE DAILY BASIS~

Always, and I mean always keep a journal because you never know when you need to look back at it for information that could possibly be handy that you don't realize it at that time. Everything from day to day needs to be written in it, specially moods that may have occurred and what may have caused that mood. Were there any horrific meltdowns and if so how where they handled? How was the individual feeling at the time? Were they sad, angry and how severe was that anger that day? What caused the anger issue and how did you handle it? Just write EVERYTHING down. What you feel isn't important may be the most important information that is needed at a later date.

~EMERGENCY SITUATIONS~

In case of an emergency situation keep the following information on file and readily available:

- In case of an emergency keep the crisis information easily available at all times in case an emergency would arise.

- Keep a record of the current medications along with the amount that is taken, and the time it is taken. Keep a record of not only the present medications, but also the past ones and the milligrams so the doctors are aware that that specific medicine was tried and didn't work.

- Keep all documents available from all healthcare providers along with a list of all appointments from the past to the present.

- If ever hospitalized keep all the hospitalization records.

~ALTERNATIVE METHODS BESIDES MEDICATION~

Remember not everyone is the same. Some individuals may see a difference with the alternative methods, besides medications and others may need the medication. This is a trial and error effect that must be tried if the individual doesn't want medicine, however it may only be half of what they need.

Besides medication, the other alternative is psychotherapy, however unless the individual's mood is stabilized the therapy will not work alone. If the individuals are hallucinating such as seeing things that are not there or hearing people that are not there, then they need the medication, it has progressed way too far.

~MOOD SWINGS~

Mood swings can shift as fast as the speed of light, especially in a child. One minute the individual can be laughing, then all of a sudden tears are falling and then they are fulfilled with excitement. The next second they can be sad and depressed that they have no idea why or what's going on. Then anger can rush through their body for no unknown reason or the very smallest thing can set them off and that's it. Their day is done because whom ever set that trigger off is done for and the day has ended for them now. Along with these feelings, they can become so overwhelmed with anxiety, that all they want to do is pace and they will nonstop worry about everything imaginable that there is. Absolutely everything!

As you get to know and understand bipolar and how the disorder affects your child or loved one, you will start noticing the triggers of what sets your child or loved one off into a frenzy. Basically, any stressful situation or anything negative in their life will affect them. These events can range from a new birth in the family, a death, family separation, to having to move. Every individual is different with what they can handle and every situation is different because what may be stressful to one, may not be stressful to another.

The stress and negativity in the individual's life can cause a disruption in their sleep patterns to where their sleep that was once needed is no longer needed. Meaning they are sleeping less or not at all. When the individual is not sleeping and you notice the difference, this is the manic stage and you will notice that they are full of energy and overly happy. After the manic stage, you will notice that this is when they will sleep and they could sleep for days, however this is not good neither because when they are sleeping this long or lounging around and wanting to be alone, this is the depressive stage and this is where suicidal tendencies may occur.

~KEEPING A ROUTINE~

With the bipolar disorder, the individual must also have a set routine that cannot be interrupted. Their routine must be kept the same as much as possible every day without interruptions. If there is a change in their routine then let them know the schedule changes ahead of time so they are aware of the change. The change may seem so small to us, however is a huge deal to them and can set them off into a frenzy and unstable state. Hard to believe, I know. Their routine must be the same. For example, their wake-up times, daily activities and especially their bed time.

~OVERSTIMULATION/MOODS~

If the individual with the bipolar disorder becomes over stimulated from their surroundings, it's almost like an individual with autism, they start shutting down. The over stimulation must be taken away. The reason why I compared the over stimulation to autism is because the same situations can over stimulate the individual with bipolar such as the house/bedroom being cluttered, certain smells for instance such as food, outside traffic or over crowded areas, different lights and certain social activities that may involve a crowd. Having too much stimulation from within the individual or outside of them can cause a mania if it becomes too overwhelming and they cannot control the situation that is occurring. Besides the mania, if the individual has certain goals set, they will not be able to complete them because the situation is too overwhelming for them and this will put them behind. Whether it's a goal for school, home, or career.

Another reason or cause for the individual to shut down and possibly move backwards instead of forwards is being bullied in school or just absolutely any type of conflicting, stressful situation. Being bullied will set the individual into a manic episode and at that time they may be unaware of what they are doing in that rage.

Besides being pushed into a mania, really what does that do to their self-confidence and their self-esteem? Yes, it pushes them down and then they feel even worse than what they already have. Even though the school systems say they have an "Anti-Bullying" policy, you know as well as I do they can't or won't control the situation until someone gets hurt whether it be emotionally of physically. I know, I have been there! I have told all of my children, you fight back, push them onto the ground if another child lays a hand on you. Maybe, then everyone will stop. Yes, I have been to the school because my children defend themselves. I just deal with it as it comes and I am their advocate and I stand behind them. I stand behind my daughter and I speak up for her when she cannot, that's what parents do.

Besides the interior and exterior events that can over stimulate the individual, so can certain foods or drinks. Caffeine and sugars can over stimulate the individual putting them into mania mode or close also. This is not something that we, as the caregiver, may think about, such as a candy bar, an iced coffee, or even an ice cream. I know I would never have imagined that the small things would set them off. I'm not into candy, however I would allow my kids to have it on the weekend as a treat.

Believe me setting my daughter off, is as if someone died! She will go on and on and on and on and on and on and on about it. Nonstop about the one subject that yes, she will drive you insane!

When these mood swings occur, what you as the parent, the loved one needs to do is record everything and I mean everything! The following is where you start with the information that is needed and more can be added in. You want to be as detailed as possible. I have listed the following to start with:

- When the mood swings started.

- What caused the mood swings?

- What was said or done at the time to cause the mood swings.

- How long did the mood swing last?

- Start a mood chart and include the stress levels, activity level, sleep schedule and eating patterns.

~WHAT IS CAUSING YOUR CHILD TO HAVE THE MOODS? ~

You need to sit down and think really hard about what is causing your child to have these mood swings. I guarantee it's not just one thing it's multiple. What's causing these mood swings? If you have kept the communication line open, then it's time to sit down with your child and discuss it. If not then it's time to start reading your child. Yes, I said reading your child! How you ask? Really easy, just a few simple steps. The first thing you need to do is start observing your child's body language. You know your child the best and you can tell by the body language if they are happy, sad, disgusted or if it's just a bunch of mood swings occurring at one time.

For example, before my daughter starts having a mania or just a bunch of mood swings I can tell not only by talking to her but also by watching her. First, she will start talking really fast and very hard to understand. Her voice will also sound different than the normal. Then she gets this abnormal twitch in her nose nonstop. Right there I know it's going to be a rough night.

~BRINGING YOUR CHILD BACK FROM THE MANIA STAGE~

You say bringing my child back from the mania stage? Can it really happen? Yes, it can with lots of patience and persistence. It is difficult, however can be done.

Let's first discuss the types of mania:

Mania which is the very intense mood of irritability where they may become hostile and euphoric at the same time. This degree of mania is mild to severe, but I do have to say good luck!

Strong Mania which is hypomania and the individual is really on edge. They are just so charged up that nothing will stop them in regards to what they want. The individual will talk about one topic to another then to another then to another and they will talk so fast that you won't be able to understand them. You will be asking them what nonstop. It is as if another personality or person has taken over. At this time, OCD (Obsessive Compulsive Disorder) will set in and they also become very giddy, giggly and loud.

Severe Mania is one where it crosses over to the psychosis state where they hallucinate and delusions occur. They are hearing voices and seeing people that really are not there.

Hypermania is where the individual just feels so amazing and nothing can take that feeling away. They feel as if they are an actress or model. The energy is forever and they are not wanting sleep at this time. They are wide awake no matter if they slept the night before or not.

Hypomania is where the individual becomes irritable and at that same time the depression sets in. No matter what you do they cannot make themselves be happy or will not find a speck of happiness. So, what do you do at this time? You've got to have an open relationship with your loved one and follow the following information:

Listen to your children, keep that communication open no matter what. Keep that communication line open weather you want to hear about what they have to say or not, listen anyways and find ways around the conversation. Listening is the most important tool to start with.

Communication is the key. Communicate openly with your children and keep it open so they will discuss everything with you. Every feeling that they have and every thought that is in their mind so you can lead them the proper way.

Encourage them to express themselves whether it be with purple hair, pink hair, blue hair, long hair, short hair, lip piercings, ring piercings, or black lipstick let it be. They are expressing themselves and need to find themselves at this time. This is an important part in their life.

If for some reason the individual will not calm down, then have them try some deep breathing exercises. Have them take a warm bath. If they are reluctant have them put some music on that they love and if not do what I do.... I hug my children and I don't let go until they calm down and I tell them how I love them and how much they mean to me over and over again.

~RAGE FROM WITHIN~

Rage can manifest itself at any time without any signs. One single disappointment with their day can set them off into a rage and their entire day is ruined. You will hear about it the entire day, maybe even for a few days depending on how devastating it was for them. As the individual goes through the rage be sure to keep any sharp or heavy objects away from them.

If there are any other children around, separate them from the area so no one gets hurt. All children that are in the household must be taught that when any time on escalation occurs they need to keep calm, leave the room and don't argue back. No matter what anyone says they will be wrong and the individual raging will always be right no matter what, at that time.

All of the children in the household must be told that when a rage occurs, get the adult in the household. The children need to know where to go to keep safe such as another room, outside, maybe a neighbor. They also must understand that if a crisis arises that have to call 911 or the crisis hotline to get a therapist on the spot as soon as possible. The crisis number should be readily available in case it is needed.

Everyone likes their household to be quiet, calm, children happy, peaceful, laid back and no fighting, however we all know that is a dream, it won't always be perfect. There will be times when you will have rage within the household and every individual needs to learn to try to adapt to it and go with the flow at times. When the individual gets into the mood that they want to argue, you will not win! As I mentioned earlier that no matter what you say to them, you will be wrong, you will never be right. They will find an answer for everything, so don't bother arguing just say "I love you" and walk away. Even though at that time, by saying "I love you" you still will not get anywhere because no matter how many times you say "I love you" or how many times you say "You're beautiful", it's not going to matter to them at that time of rage. They won't believe you and they will not care. They just want to argue and don't feed into that negativity because they enjoy it. Heck don't even look at them! If you look at them they are going to ask you what or why are staring at me, when you're not. At the time of rage, they feel that they are ugly, no matter what they do is no good, and that no one loves them. Even though the individual doesn't want to hear it I always say, "I love you and always will no matter what. You are a very beautiful, intelligent girl and when you decide you want to talk without arguing come find me." Then I walk away and go on about my day until she decides she wants to discuss what's going on.

~WHAT MAY BRING ON A MANIA EPISODE? ~

Mania can be brought on by many of our senses that no one else may think of. When it comes to the senses of a bipolar individual it's almost like an autism spectrum disorder. Many things may trigger a mania that us as an individual take advantage of everyday such as certain smells, too much stimuli such as noise, certain places, lighting or certain objects they have seen.

VISUAL/AUDITORY STIMULI

Certain things that are seen whether it be a color, certain object or too many people can cause an individual to enter a mania episode whether it be big or small. A busy scene can bring on a mania due to their anxiety level. A noisy place can also bring on a mania due to them being very sensitive to their surroundings along with the lighting of an area, whether it be too much light or too little of light, every individual is different.

If any of these situations cause a mania get the individual into a quiet area to calm down. Teach the individual how to deal with difficult situations when they feel anxiety coming on such as some breathing techniques or even EFT tapping to help them cope with their surroundings. I will explain what EFT is in the next few sections.

~PARANOIA ~

When an individual is in a paranoia state, they become anxious and delusional. One with paranoia may think that everyone is talking about them such as whispering behind their back and starring at that them when in actuality none of that is actually happening. At some point, they think that everyone is against them. It is a scary thought of that actually happening. Could you imagine what that is like? No, I couldn't at all. I couldn't imagine dealing with that anytime.

Believe me when I say I have. It's difficult to sit back and watch your loved one go through this and there isn't anything that you can do at that time except try to assure them that no one is talking about them. All I could say is "I love you and care about you more than anything in this world." I always hugged her even though I was getting pushed away. I made sure I recorded everything in my journal so the doctor could be updated. The sad part is not only watching your child or loved one hurt, but the care giver hurts also, not physically but emotionally. When you are getting pushed away from your own child, even though they are not themselves at that time, it still hurts. I remember there where days I would sit and cry and pray that I would get my caring and loving daughter back. I wanted her the way she used to be and always asked why?

~BE AWARE WHEN MANIA OCCURS~

Be aware when the mania occurs and pay attention for the length of time. If the individual thinks and or believes that everyone is talking about them and starring at them and this doesn't subside without them coming back to reality, then they may have that feeling that someone is coming after them. They may think that someone is out to get them, that everyone is against them. If the individual believes any of these things listed is occurring then they may harm others because at this time they are fearful of harm and someone is going to hurt them that they will harm the individual (s) to keep themselves or their family safe.

When my daughter was going through the manias and I was unaware at the time because she was afraid to tell me. She was afraid to tell me for fear I would think she was crazy, even though I always kept the communication open between us. My daughter didn't tell me right away so the bipolar disorder became worse to where she was seeing things that happened even though it actually in reality didn't happen. Sounds confusing but just follow me here.

There were times my daughter would see a lady just standing there staring at her or she would be walking down the street and this lady would appear right in front of her and my daughter would run because she was afraid. Mind you this lady never existed, this was part of the mania. How did I find out? My daughter finally had enough courage to tell me, however she didn't realize there was more that she was seeing that didn't really exist and I wish she would have told me sooner before it got out of hand. Come to find out she was seeing me, the parent, the one that loves her and will always do anything for her, cursing at her, telling her that she was worthless, no good and throwing shoes at her. Why you ask? When the mania starts and they start hallucinating it's normally the loved ones that they attack either emotionally, physically or the individual sees them hurting them even though it never happened. Watching your child go through this, hurts more than anything imaginable because you can't just take it away like you would love to do. I don't know how many times I would say "Please God take it away from my daughter and give it to me."

~DEPRESSION OR THE WINTER BLUES? ~

Believe it or not depression is the first sign of bipolar. If you are unaware of the first signs, yes, you will miss the sign. At first you will think it's depression because all of the depressed signs are there, however as a parent you will say, "No, not my child. They have a family that loves them and will do anything for them. Why would they be depressed? No way! That's not it."

The signs for depression are as follows:

- The child will be withdrawn

- The child will lose weight or even possibly gain weight (Everyone is different)

- They will crave carbohydrates and sugar insanely. One example is nonstop ice cream

- The individual feels helpless

- Insomnia will kick in because they feel as if they don't need to sleep

- The individual will sleep in the middle of the day and towards evening

- All activities they use to do have ceased

- Their concentration is very poor, unable to cope

- The individual says that they don't want to live anymore. They feel that they don't have a purpose in life. They have the urge of wanting to die. They say that they wish they were never born.

- Self-mutilation such as cutting

~WHAT HAPPENS WHEN MANIA AND DEPRESSION OCCUR? ~

This is when the fun begins! Not exactly. The world wind of fire starts. Not what anyone wants to go through but it isn't something that we can ever stop, but just learn how to adjust it.

Irritability is a huge occurrence and it can't be stopped until we learn what's causing it and try to stay away from it or learn how to adjust to it. It's difficult to see your child go through irritable moods and there isn't anything you can do to make it better or to make them happy. No matter what you do, doesn't help at the time. Irritability is very common in the manic and depressive phases.

You may ask what exactly is irritability? Irritability is when an individual with bipolar disorder can come in many forms such hostility, impatient, confusion, aches and can also be seen in the mania, hypomania and the depression that occurs.

Like mentioned in the earlier sections, certain smells, sounds and light can be very overloading for the individual with bipolar and this will cause anger and rage within them. They aren't sure how to deal with it or what is causing it at the time.

Depression comes with the irritability and depression can also be part of the individual's disorder which is also known as a manic depression because the individual's mood can alternate rapidly from their highs and lows. The depression can last for hours, days, weeks or months. Children tend to have rapid changes that can last for few hours and it repeats itself without the proper treatment.

What I found that has worked, get the individual away from the situation that is causing the irritability or the depressed mood that is distracting the child. Mom becomes the most annoying individual or the most embarrassing individual while out in public if needed. I will sing, (which is awful, my children don't want me to sing in public) dance, joke around or make fun of everything possible to distract my child and make her laugh to forget about the circumstance that is causing the irritability or depression. I will make myself look like a fool if I need to. I don't care what others think of me as long as my child is happy, laughing and enjoying life.

Exercise is fantastic for depression, irritability and even the individual's confidence, self-esteem and of course overall health. Exercise releases the serotonin and the endorphins which the fantastic, feel good feeling, that rush you get after exercising, that huge release of tension and lots of energy afterwards. Exercise can be as simple as taking a walk, releasing tension into a punching bag, running, lifting weights or even something as simple as yoga.

~ONCE THE MOOD SUBSIDES~

Once the roller coaster ride is completed for the minutes, hours or days and the rage from within has subsided, the individual can be happy, smile, joke, laugh, engage in life, enjoy everything around them and enjoy the love that you give them. It is fantastic to see your child to enjoy the simplest things in life once again. There is nothing in this world that compares to having your child back to reality and be themselves once again, or as close as it gets.

~THE ADVOCATE NEEDS DESTRESSED TOO! ~

Through the times of need, the loved one that takes care of the individual needs time away, a time for themselves, a time to destress also. The risk of the advocate or caretaker to end up with PTSD is very high with the roller coaster rides that occur. PTSD, is Post Traumatic Stress Disorder and comes with the stress, physical exhaustion and the part of feeling guilty because the caregiver blames themselves for what their loved one is going through.

The individual needs to find a way to handle their own stress because after taking care of an individual with bipolar, yes there is a time that the stress becomes so high that they don't know how much more they can handle and they need to destress themselves in order to take good care of their loved one. At times, I do become stressed, overwhelmed, depressed, and even fear of losing the loved one builds up inside and I am not sure of what to do. Being a mother, you are always supposed to know what to do because you are mom. The way I handle stress almost all of the time is through exercise. I love exercise because I feel so destressed, relaxed, energized and the rush afterwards is just an awesome feeling. I get the feeling that I can handle anything that comes my way! I enjoy walks with my daughter, meditating in the morning before I face my day, throwing an exercise video in and moving with that, to get my day started. Throughout the day, I listen to positive affirmations to keep me feeling positive and I have learned to do EFT (which we discussed in the earlier section) when my anxiety becomes high so I can calm down and tackle anything that comes my way. I have learned ways to release the negativity that tackled my family, ways to destress and let all of the emotions go so I am not so overwhelmed. Who wants to carry negativity with them throughout the day? I sure don't.

Some other ways of destressing if you're not into exercise is finding the happy place for yourself, whether it be taking time for yourself to soak in a warm bath to relax by candlelight with a glass of wine. Finding that close friend that you trust to talk to, we all need some time to vent. Spending time with your pet which is the best therapy ever because they always listen, will not talk back and will always love you unconditionally. No matter what it is that you choose, make your time for yourself and yourself only. You need the relaxation because if you don't take care of yourself how are you going to take care of others? You can't!

~JOURNALING~

As much as you think, you can't remember everything as it comes down to it, you really can't. You can't remember all of the important facts like you want, and what you may think isn't important, just may be the most important. What I have learned on my own is write everything down and I mean everything! This journal is going to help you and your child out in the long run. It is well worth taking a few minutes out of your day to complete. In order to receive proper treatment all facts must be accurate.

~TREATING BIPOLAR DISORDER~

Treating bipolar sounds so easy as just giving an individual a pill, however it isn't. I wish treatment was just that easy, then not only would my life would be so simple, but so would my daughters.

The hardest part is diagnosing bipolar at a young age, or should I say finding a doctor that will diagnose it at a young age because normally doctors don't want to diagnose it until the individual is their 20's or 30's. It's later in life that doctors want to diagnose it, when really it needs to be diagnosed early to get the individual help before it becomes worse and they don't realize what they are doing because it seems so normal to them.

Treating bipolar is a combination of therapy and medication. Therapy is a definite and they need this at least once a week or they cannot cope with their everyday life. They need to vent their rage to someone else besides their loved one because they don't want to hurt the loved one any more than they feel that they already have. Therapy not only gives the individual time to vent their rage but to also retrain their thought process in everyday situations. Then not only is the therapy important but also the medication that they are prescribed. Finding the proper medication is just as difficult and important as therapy. Believe I know from experience because we went through different medications. I wasn't sure if we would get it right. It was scary at the time. I knew if a medicine didn't work things would get worse. Anyone could have gotten hurt whether it be herself or a family member if she got upset enough.

The most important part is not only the therapy and medication but also you as a parent to monitor your child since you are the one that knows them the best. Monitoring your child means keep the journaling going, keep the communication line open, watch for any behavioral issues and mood swings along with for any self-mutilation that may occur. When it comes to self-mutilation watch not only their arms, but their toes, and thigh areas because they will try to hide it from you. Not only do you watch for cutting but also scratching. Just because they self-mutilate doesn't always mean they want to die, sometimes it's a cry for help or a way they take the rage out and it makes them feel better.

Regarding mood swings, you are looking for the highs and lows, the minor irritability to a very high irritability. The mood swings can occur at any given time and it even includes an evil look. Sometimes I would say if the looks could kill me I would have been dead. The eyes can be so cold with no life in them and it is the scariest to see with your own child. I always prayed that I would get my girl back because I could see the pain in her eyes. I would cry for days while she was going through this.

You will also be looking to monitor the depression. They seem to be okay for a while and then it may slowly creep back in. Their energy level will be low, this is a big clue. They will want to sleep all day long, even when the sun is shining and it's the most beautiful day outside.

Mania phase is another sign that you will be looking for. Regarding mania, you will be watching for them to not wanting to sleep all day or all night, running around like wild fire working on not only one but several projects at one time. When they are communicating with you during a mania, they will ramble on nonstop not only about one topic, but several at one time, and their speech is difficult to understand because they will be talking so fast you won't be able to understand them right away.

Also, watch for psychological disturbances such as are they seeing things that are not there or hearing things or voices that are not there?

Basically, to be safe and you are unsure just document everything about their day, everything! All this information will come in handy when discussing care to the doctor or therapist.

~ACCEPTANCE~

Once the proper medication is found, therapy is on a regular basis, and the household is once again stable and no one under stress like an emotional rollercoaster, then acceptance needs to take place. Acceptance must happen with the parent and the child. If acceptance doesn't occur, then everyone is going to fight the situation and the individual will not receive all the help that is there for them. Not only does the individual diagnosed need the assistance but so does the entire family. Once acceptance occurs, then the family can start living a life they once had together once again. The family must also learn coping skills just as the diagnosed individual. Everyone must work together. What happened in the past must be forgiven and the individual needs everyone's support and love from within.

~THE HATED THOUGHT AS A PARENT~

Being a parent, we never think about having to put our children on medicine, at least not for psychiatric illnesses. This is a huge decision to make at such a young age! You ponder upon it to make sure that you are making the right decision. Decisions, decisions, decisions...what do I do? Hmm.... If I don't put my child on medication, then they can have psychosis if they don't already. They could hurt themselves or someone else. If I do put them on it then they may not be the same person they once were, but they really aren't now neither. They could become overly medicated. What do I do, you ask yourself? Honestly you may never get that same child back ever again. You may have to get to know and understand this new child that has been brought to you due to this disorder. As much as it hurts, it's the truth. It will be a struggle for the both of you because they may not know themselves neither at this time and they may be afraid of themselves also.

Think about it once, the proper medication will stabilize the individual's mood and take away the manic episodes that they are having. Honestly the depression and anxiety will always be there somewhere even if it's in the back of their mind. Only the individual suffering can find that one thing to make them happy and to deal with the anxiety. You, as a parent can help by suggesting some activities that will bring enjoyment and maybe give them that slight push into it and not let them quit that activity no matter what. We just hope as a parent that we are doing the right thing at that time. Give it some time and you will know for sure. Just keep everything positive for them such as listening to positive affirmations every day. What you hear and if you hear it enough you will eventually believe.

~DAILY LIFE~

When it comes to having a child that is bipolar or even as an adult having a regular routine is very crucial in their daily life. First of all, a bipolar child cannot control all of their emotions. One is because they are unsure of them at that time. They cannot control their own moods at all times specially when they feel that they lost control of everything. They need to feel as if they are in control somewhat of their own life and this includes to waking up the same time every day. Let them set an alarm to wake up so they feel that they are in control, and let them decide what they want to wear for that day even if you don't completely agree 100%. Go with the flow and let them experiment a bit, even if its letting them wear that make up that you don't care too much for. If they feel that they are not in control, at least a little, then this will cause a rage, mood swings, depression, anxiety and even a mania episode. Establish a regular routine with your child so they have that stability in their life that they need the most.

Make a regular schedule for them and discuss their routine with them so they know what is expected. If there is a change in their routine, tell them ahead of time, so they know what to expect. Give them that control in their life. Remind them daily if there are changes that may occur such as a doctor appointment or whatever it is that day that may throw them off.

~CHANGES THAT MAY OCCUR WITHIN THEIR LIFE~

If there is a change coming and you know it for sure, let them aware of it ahead of time so they are expecting that change so you don't mess with their regular routine and throw them off completely. The change can be anything from a school routine, moving, vacations, appointments, it doesn't matter, communicate with your child, they need it.

Most individuals with bipolar are slow with change and despise it, so they need to be aware in advance.

~STRUCTURE ISN'T ALWAYS THE ISSUE~

You can note that everything will not be easy even the changes that occur in life. No matter how much you may have a routine set and keep their life structured there may be a day that it doesn't matter to them. They may decide to react differently all of a sudden and that no matter what you say he or she will not listen to you. You will feel as though you are talking to a brick wall. In fact, you may get more reaction from that brick wall. Yes, you will get frustrated most defiantly. Just remember that this is not your child at that time.

There could be other issues or circumstances causing your child to act out and they may not even be aware that they are acting out. You ask what could be causing this? Many things could be causing these situations such as:

- The lighting that surrounds them

- Certain smells

- The atmosphere that surrounds them

- Amount of people around (is it too busy for them)

All of this matters to them because they become so involved in their emotions at that specific time that they cannot change how they feel or their reactions at that time. They get so involved in how they feel that they cannot respond positively no matter what they do. I can tell you threatening them with a punishment is not going to help anything but make it worse. Threatening them with a punishment will only cause mood swings to become out of control and chaos will occur within the entire family. All the child is going to do is defy you at that time, don't make it any worse on them than what it is.

You, the parent, will understand your child and know the difference of when they are not listening to you because they don't want to or because they are unstable at that time. No matter what medicine the individual is on you will still go through manias or behavioral issues at times due to too much going on in their surroundings.

Your child must understand and realize when they are unstable, what's causing it and so they can communicate it to you so you can get them out of that situation as fast as possible. Let the child know what was occurring and how they were acting at that time so they can learn what is going on if they are unaware. They can then communicate it to you if it happens again. This is why I keep open communication and relationship with my child. I want to know everything that's going on so I can help or at least try to help. When certain events happen in their life I guarantee that they don't even realize everything that is going on. They just get that rush of emotions of fear, anxiety, depression and hatred all at once.

~CALMING/COPING TECHNIQUES~

Calming techniques that are listed in this section are not just for your child but you as a parent, caregiver, can use these also.

107

BREATHING EXERCISE

Breathing exercises are an excellent way to calm down and makes you feel rejuvenated. Breathing exercises can release the tension and anxiety that you are feeling inside.

For the breathing techniques follow the following directions:

1. First, take a slow breath in and inhale counting to four

2. Hold a breath for a second

3. Then exhale slowly for a count of eight. When exhaling make sure to breath all of the air out slowly.

4. Repeat as needed until you feel calm and the tension is lifting away.

MEDITATION

Meditation is another excellent way to start your day and to end it. Mediation can be done anywhere, anytime, and you only need five minutes to feel refreshed and relaxed. Meditation can be done while in bed, sitting on your couch, or even sitting in your vehicle. Meditation videos can be found on the world-wide web such as YouTube. Meditation is great for starting your day, relaxing or even to feel refreshed.

To get you started I have an example to follow if you would like.

1. Find a quiet spot and make sure you won't have any interruptions.

2. Sit quietly, make sure you are in a comfortable position and close your eyes.

3. Breath normal at this time, however notice your breaths.

4. Once you notice your breaths, slowly take a deep breath in and slowly let it out and repeat. Notice your inhales and exhales.

5. Concentrating on your breathing, will help ease your mind and allow all your thoughts to move to the side.

6. Clear your mind of all thoughts and concentrate on the most beautiful place that you would like to be. For instance, maybe feel the sun shining down on you, feel the warmth. Imagine a huge field of the most beautiful flowers and maybe your running through them and enjoying the nature.

7. When you notice a random thought poking in, throw it to the side and come back to where you were.

8. Just relax, enjoy the moments of peacefulness and release that tension with any negative thoughts that you may have.

POSITIVE AFFIRMATIONS

Positive affirmations are another way to calm down or to feel positive throughout the day. Positive affirmations are based upon a specific negative thought or situation. Affirmations help you to stop the negative thoughts and to stop the self- sabotage in your life. They help you to visualize and to believe that there is a positive outcome or outlook on a specific situation. They also help you to believe that you can do or succeed at anything you put your mind to. These can also be found on the world-wide web such as YouTube.

EMOTIONAL FREEDOM TAPPING (EFT)

EFT which stands for Emotional Freedom Tapping is a great way to help calm down, relax and to really think about how you feel. Take that negative feeling or situation and turn it into a positive thought. This can be found on the world-wide web also.

To get you started I have directions listed to give you an idea of how it works.

When you are feeling anxious, depressed, stressed or generally upset, what is the underlying issue? Identify your problem from within.

How do you feel about that issue or situation? Rate the intensity of that problem with zero being the lowest level and ten being the highest.

Acknowledge the problem, then follow with a positive affirmation. For example, we will use depression. Such as: "Even though I am depressed, I accept myself." "Even though I am depressed because I didn't get the job, I completely accept myself." "Even though I am feeling sad and upset about this job, I truly accept myself."

Perform the following tapping technique:

1. With four fingers on one hand, tap the karate chop area on your hand. This is the outer edge of your hand and the opposite side from the thumb.

2. Repeat your statement three times while tapping the karate chop area and take a deep breath. (The setup statement is "Even though I am depressed, I accept myself")

There is more in regards to tapping and I will go into some more detail, however the karate chop area is the best place to begin. When you are in public and feel the need to tap whether it be for depression, anxiety, etc. the easiest and less obvious place is the karate chop area. No one will realize what you are doing and at the same time you are feeling at ease.

Tapping Pressure Points Used

Besides the karate chop area there are eight other pressure points used. While tapping this pressure points two fingers are used for these areas.

- The center top of your head

- The inner edge of your eyebrow close to your nose

- Your temple close to your eye

- Close to your cheek bone right under your eye

- Between your nose and your lip

- Your chin, the middle part

- Your collarbone where there is a ridge.

- Right under your arm about three to four inches from your armpit.

Once these areas are used as pressure points one time around a full cycle, then the cycle is repeated from the beginning while saying the negative situation phrase. The phrase can be replaced with anything that you would like to work on. The cycle can be repeated as many times as you like until the depression, anxiety, etc. is relieved. Once the negative situation is gone, replace it with positive feedback.

Positive phrases that can be used.

- I have the ability to overcome depression.

- I have the ability to overcome anxiety.

- I am willing to change and am excited about the new me.

- I am enjoying the peace from within myself.

- I love me and whom I am.

The phrases used are only examples. You can use any phrase that you like and feel comfortable with.

~COMMUNICATION~

As in any relationship communication is the key between you and your child. Keep those communication lines open at all times, even if you don't like what you hear. I know I want to know what my child is doing at all times, how she feels or what's on her mind. As I have told all of my children, I may not like what I hear, but it's okay, because I will deal with it on my own. I know you, as a parent/caregiver, reading this want to know what your child is doing, how they feel or what they may be up to and thinking about. The only way to do this is by listening and communicating. This is especially important if at one time they have or may even have a chance to enter into a psychosis. With psychosis, this where they will see things that are not there and even hear voices that are not there, telling them to do things that they would never normally do.

~EMPATHY~

Emphasize with your child and let them know that you do understand and that you will always be understanding. Children need to know that you understand what they are going through so they feel safe telling you. I, myself can emphasize with my daughter not only because I have studied the healthcare field and psychology but I can also really emphasize with the depression. I suffer from depression every day, I have suffered for years. When I say, I understand, I really do! Unlike most I cannot take medications for it because it makes it worse so I have learned to live with it on my own. The calming techniques I listed also work for depression, so I have not listed anything that I have not tried with my daughter or myself that hasn't worked.

~POST-TRAUMATIC STRESS DISORDER~

In fact, parents that are taking care of children with bipolar are known to suffer from post-traumatic stress disorder, in which develops from coping on a daily basis with a child that has extreme moods. Extreme mood swings can occur just as easy as an individual can tell your child "No."

~KEEPING A ROUTINE WITH YOUR CHILD~

Yes, as I have explained it is very important to keep a regular routine with your child to lessen the stress in their life.

When it comes to a morning routine, this is the most important because this is how the day is started. One change they are not aware of will devastate their entire day. Mornings are the most difficult I have found personally, however once the individual becomes use to a regular routine, waking up at the same time, eating at the same time, it becomes easier. The individual becomes use to it and doesn't even think about it unless there is something, anything that throws it off, the smallest minute or second will wreck their entire day.

There are times that the individual is exhausted, not just physically, but mentally and they don't want to crawl out of bed to face the day. Especially if there isn't any sunshine or its winter, cold, and dreary outside. I can't say I don't blame them at all. Sometimes getting out of bed is a huge chore for them. Don't nag them to wake up, ease them into waking up such as using a countdown method such as "Good morning, time to wake up. You have 15 minutes." Again, "Good morning, time to wake up. You have 10 minutes." Go from there. A countdown normally helps them to become motivated.

~REFUSAL TO ATTEND SCHOOL~

Yes, it will get to a point that the child will not want to attend school. Yes, they have done fantastic, their grades are great, however do they have any friends anymore like they once had? Your answer is more than likely going to be no. Yes, the child has changed and so has everyone else around them. The individual isn't as close to friends as they use to be, they become withdrawn because yes, they have changed and now the other children are now making fun of them. Maybe the way the child's dress changes because they are trying to find themselves and other children are making fun of them. Your child at this point isn't into socializing like they once were due to their anxiety. As I have been told from my daughter, she is told that she is different. No one likes her because she doesn't want to talk to them anymore or because now she dresses differently. She is called EMO. Emo, really, why you ask? All because she enjoys expressing herself with band t shirts. She doesn't care for dresses or bright colors, she enjoys her jeans and band shirts. Well, heck, I enjoy wearing the same type of clothing. So, guess that would make me "emo" huh? Nope, that makes myself or her happy dressing casual and comfortable.

~FEELINGS AFTER SCHOOL~

Feelings after school are going to vary depending on how the teachers, school staff and other children treated them throughout the day. Not only looking on how others treated them, their day also depends on any schedule changes that may have occurred that they were unaware of ahead of time.

After school, their anxiety may be so high that they themselves cannot control it. What they need at this time is the parent, caretaker, loved one to sit down and listen to them, listen about their day. Let them get it all out, the good and bad, so they feel better. Even if you don't understand it all, listen to them. All they need is that extra support, that extra ear. Just sit back and listen to their entire day. Whether it be the good or bad listen to what they have to say and how they handled it. You may be able to give some positive input into their day and that may be all they want or need.

~SYMPATHETIC OR UNSTABLE~

When a child is feeling sympathetic or is unstable at the time, it is very difficult to take them anywhere out of their comfort zone, which would be their house. Their house is their sanctuary, their comfort zone, that is their everything. It may be difficult taking them to a crowded place or a brightly lit place. When this happens this when the individual and parent must find ways to keep them calm. Heck, go back a few sections to reread calming techniques. Here's a list of a few situations that may set them off at the time.

Huge crowds: Heading into a crowded store, restaurant or any tightly enclosed area. Sit or stand on the outside of the crowd or inside in an empty area until you can calm down enough to join in. Once in a desolated area, find certain areas of that room that you can point out in case an attack occurs. This one area is where you can walk to in order to calm down. Once you pick these key areas out and slowly mingle out into the crowd, you will be okay. Remember, if you can take a friend for support that little bit of support helps a lot. Remember, you as the parent or caregiver are the child's safe place so they will feel comfortable with you. One thing my daughter has learned to do on her own, since she has a phone and normally listens to her music, when we go out in public and her anxiety kicks in she puts her earbuds in her ears. She's not listening to music, but the earbuds actually eliminates some of the sound for her which relaxes her and she's able to concentrate in crowded places.

Too much noise: Here is another instance where the earbuds would come in handy or even earplugs to block out the excessive noise.

Bright light: Individuals with bipolar cannot stand bright lights including the sunshine. We always carry sunglasses around, even if she needs them inside.

Emotional situations are places that are the most difficult for them, especially with their hypersensitivity because they become overwhelmed and can't handle it very well. It's way too much at one time for them. In these cases, either away or at home, we as a parent and child must find ways to handle the emotions. A few ways that I have found that works is:

- Having a punching bag available and letting them take their frustrations out on it.

- Let them go out for a bike ride and run their frustrations out.

- Cardio is the best, exercise is a great stress reliever.

- Enrolling the individual into martial arts is another great way to handle emotions because it not only releases the stress and anxiety, but also builds their self-confidence and teaches discipline

- Taking the child to a playground is another great way to release energy and let them run, run and run!

- A great way to relax is swimming. The water is so relaxing and calming to the soul and body.

- Wanting to find a place to rejuvenate, the library is fantastic! The library is quiet and you can visit any place in the world for free or be anyone you want to be. All you have to do is find the book that you enjoy and off you go. You can come back to reality anytime you want.

- Having a pet is also fantastic. A pet is such great therapy and releases stress. Anytime you don't feel loved, snuggle to a pet and they will give you all the love in the world. As the say a dog is a mankind's best friend.

- Another great way to relax on your own and set your emotions free is listening to music that you enjoy the most.

- As I have mentioned earlier in the book is meditation.

- Breathing techniques will also be helpful in helping with emotions and stressful situations.

- There is nothing like home, their safe heaven. This is where they feel relaxed, calm and this is their place. No one can hurt them because it's theirs and you are also there with them. There is not any reason to feel emotional, afraid or anxiety.

~LET'S QUIET DOWN FOR BEDTIME~

Yeah okay! This can be so much easier said than done. Bedtime can be an anxious time because they can be full of energy or uncertainty. Uncertain on what tomorrow will bring. This is where the mania, depression, and anxiety presents itself at night and they are unaware of it. The mania will also be accompanied with an obsessive-compulsive behavior.

The best thing that can be done is to establish a set bedtime and routine.

~PULLING IT ALL TOGETHER ~

There is nothing worse than losing your child or coming close to it. I did lose my daughter for a while there. She wasn't physically gone, however with the chemical imbalance, she was not herself, the kind caring girl that loved life and was full of laughter no longer existed. I wasn't sure if I would ever get her back. A part of me was gone with her.

After almost a year, I have her back! Happy, full of life again and more confident than ever!

She has her laughter, sense of humor, kindness, loving life and don't mess with me attitude. I absolutely love it!

I could have lost her to the bipolar disorder forever if the signs and symptoms weren't caught. I could also have lost her to the suicidal tendencies or risky behaviors that were occurring.

I love my daughter very much and could never live a day without her. No matter what, I will always be right beside her, cheering her on, loving her, advocating for her and doing whatever it is I have to do to keep her moving forward to have the great life that she is supposed to have. ***That's what mom's do!***

Hopefully the researched that I provided and real-life events that occurred on how I learned and what I went through helps you or a loved one in the journey. I know it took courage to pick this book up and decide to read it. Specially if you're not sure that the child or loved one has a diagnosis of bipolar disorder and you're researching for answers, symptoms or similarities. Hopefully this book was able to assist in answering some of your questions or point you into the right direction.

If you or a love one has the diagnoses with bipolar, hopefully you realize that you are not the only one out there with it. You are not alone. There is help, there is support, there are others alike. You just need to reach out for the help or guidance. Accept what you have been diagnosed with, research everything you can about it. The learning process never stops.

~Acknowledgments~

I want to say thank you to my wonderful editor, Alissa Ashlock, for taking the time out of her busy schedule to assist me with this book. I could never have done it without you!

I also want to thank my family and close friends Pam Webb and Amber Rhode for believing in me.

The one I want to really thank is no longer with me, she passed away right before I completed this book and that is my mom, Sharon Collar. Sharon pushed me and said, "You can do anything you put your mind to." She was right. I just wish she was here to read it. Most importantly she was here for the guidance when I needed her the most. She listened and guided me through the challenges that came my way with my daughter, no matter what time of day it was.

About the Author

Writing is about passion and researching! My drive is writing and teaching others what I have learned. My enjoyment is writing about the medical field, in which I have a Master's degree in. The knowledge is never ending within the field. Technology is always changing along with studies regarding psychological disorders.

I truly can relate to many of the psychological disorders on a personal level and I am truly passionate about them. My writing not only comes from research but also from hands- on experience. I am able to put myself in the other individual's shoes and empathize with them.

It's not only the individual with the disorder that hurts, it's the loved ones that take care of them also. It hurts to see a loved one hurting emotionally or physically, not understanding why they feel the way they do. I know from being there, however, the more knowledge that you have, the more you can understand and the more you can help others.

My favorite place to go and spend time is at the library, where I have the entire world at my fingertips! I can go anywhere, do anything, and be whomever I want! Knowledge is the key to success and understanding the world!

Are You Awake, Yet?

Made in the USA
San Bernardino, CA
06 December 2017